MY LIFE, MY STORY, MY LEGACY

VINTAGE WIT AND WISDOM

Stories collected by Danni Burton

LITTLE WHITE DOG PRESS

Copyright © 2015 Danni Burton

All rights reserved. No part of this book may be reproduced, stored in a retrieval system or transmitted in any form or by any means without the prior written consent of the publisher, except by a reviewer who may quote brief passages in a review to be printed in a newspaper, magazine, blog, or journal. Requests for permission should be sent to:

Little White Dog Press:
info@littlewhitedogpress.com

Cover Design: Tony Portillo
Illustrations: Terje Nordberg

This book is a compilation of short stories and memoirs. This book contains autobiographical elements about its various authors. The voices and colloquialisms of the individual storytellers were honored throughout the book. The authors have made every attempt to recreate events, locales, and conversations from their memories of them. In order to maintain their anonymity, the authors may have changed or may have left out the names of individuals, places, and identifying characteristics and details such as physical properties, occupations, and places of residence.

PUBLISHED BY LITTLE WHITE DOG PRESS

ISBN-10: 0996295518
ISBN-13: 978-0-9962955-1-2
First Edition

IN LOVING MEMORY

This book is dedicated to Mom and Dad, Grama Mary, Nana, Aunt Jean and Uncle Nels, and my sister Heather.

They were all great and funny storytellers who often regaled me with the tales of our Scottish ancestors and many of their own secret adventures.

How could that shy little girl who loved stories not become a Scottish Storyteller? My time with them has truly shaped my life.

They have all left my life—some way too early. But their memories live on as treasures.

TABLE OF CONTENTS

Fiddlin' Around 1

My Special Blue-covered Pillow 3

A Helmet, Drugs, and Redemption 4

The Wake-up Call...the Challenges...and the Gifts 6

Bananas 8

My Angel From Heaven 10

Unplanned New Life 11

Clean and Shiny! 13

Pies 15

A Miracle in Alaska 16

Values Shared Through Generations 18

Hanging on Through the Bumps of Life 19

Riches Money Can't Buy 21

Sister June...the Entrepreneur 22

Sticks! 24

Teaching and Learning in the Peace Corp 25

The Gold Key and the Silver Key 27

Rocks, Stones, Bricks...And People 29

It's the Inner Beauty that Counts 31

Three Goals I Set...and Met 32

A Simple Phrase...Welcome Home 34

When in Doubt...Stick Together 36

Sixty and Just Getting Started 37

Do Your Homework and Be Prepared 39

Caring and Being Cared For 40

Grandma Rose 42

A Simple Scottish Story	43
What I Teach and What I Learn	45
Don't Put All Your Apples in One Basket	46
Burying the Hatchet	48
The Compass that Guides Us	50
The Magic of Books	52
Turning Dirty into $$$$	54
Caring Beyond Our Duty	56
The Village Raised the Child	58
How I Now Inspire…as I was Inspired	60
Do What You Love…Love What You Do	62
You Can Do It!	64
Follow Your Star!	66
Up, Down, and Back Up Again	68
How a Fire Started My Career	70
Two Souls Crossing Paths	72
Let's Dance	74
Gaga, Poppoo…and Mae	76
The Many Twists and Turns on the Way to Becoming a Teacher	78
Looking Back at 105	80
How a Visit Turned a Life Around	82
Let Me Entertain You	83
You Step Into Your Power When You Hit the Drum	85
If You Want It…Find the Way!	87
I Always Wanted to Be A Doctor	88
Trinidad Mama	90
Precious Moments	92
Acknowledgements	93
About the Author	94

INTRODUCTION

As I traveled throughout the world, I gathered tales from amazing storytellers in many places, countries, and languages.

I have sat on rocks, stood on bridges, and joined the locals at the pub to visit and learn from many vintage people. Among them were a Chinese wiseman, Maori historian, Hawaiian shaman, Scottish comedian, and Creole fortuneteller.

My mother used to say, "People are like books. If you don't open the cover, you miss the story."

When I became a vintage person, I wanted to find a way for others to share their history, wit, and wisdom with younger generations.

So, I began this project, which involved interviewing and gathering stories from people ages 55 to 105, from many cultures, languages, and life experiences.

I am gifting books to shelters, rehab centers, schools, and hospitals so these wonderful stories can offer hope, inspiration, and encouragement to others as they go through challenging times.

Enjoy!

—*The Scottish Storyteller*

FIDDLIN' AROUND

I received a traditional classical music education, and today I am a performing musician and violin, viola, and fiddle teacher. I have learned to be flexible and think outside the box. When I teach, the lesson may not be about music, but about kindling a spark or just having fun.

One of my students, Merina, was an exuberant child who loved animals and moved constantly. As a long-time family friend I became her music teacher. We began with family activity lessons with her sister Sarah and friend Timothy and then went on to individual music and violin lessons.

One time five-year-old Merina would not come out of the bathroom. For our music lesson that day, we looked in the mirror while she drew music notes on her cheeks with face paint.

Another day the tumbling mat arrived, and tumbling and cartwheels had her attention.

So, each crease in the mat became a line of the music staff, and she tumbled her way through scales, singing her violin tunes, jumping from note to note on the imaginary music staff.

On the day new little chicks arrived, her attention was riveted on them. We drew a large music staff on a piece of paper, put it in the bottom of the pen, and when a dropping fell on the staff, we played that note.

It became the game of how many ways to play the violin—backwards, sideways, and even upside down. She played while walking, skipping, twirling, and balancing on rocks and benches.

One day she asked if it were possible to play the violin and piano at the same time. She stood barefoot on the piano bench and balanced on her left foot. Then she gently selected keys on the piano with her right big toe and played the same note on her violin.

Another time she was sitting in a tree and would not come down, so I handed her the violin, and with her in the tree and me on the ground we played her entire repertoire of music together. It was the first lesson where she stayed in one place. And she was up in a tree!

My job is simply to be flexible and introduce the violin and fiddle in a joyous way, even if the student is not interested.

Eighteen years ago Merina, Sarah, Timothy, and I started this music adventure together. Today Sarah is a nurse, Timothy a fireman, and Merina graduated with a major in music!

—*Lee Anne, teaching, fiddlin', and having fun*

MY SPECIAL BLUE-COVERED PILLOW

It was the winter of 2002, and my son had passed away. The weather was cold and rainy, and I felt chilled. I was on a bus that was approaching the stop where I needed to change buses. I got off, and it moved on. And then I realized that I had left my special blue-covered pillow on that bus.

This special pillow helped my back be comfortable while I was sitting. So I felt angry with myself for being so forgetful and leaving it behind.

Suddenly another bus pulled up, stopped, and a wheelchair was lowered in front. In the wheelchair was a young man with a crippled body. He was all bundled up and wore a Christmas hat. He had a big smile on his face and a twinkle in his shining blue eyes. I stared at that beautiful smile.

And then I asked myself how I could be sad when I had lost a pillow and he had lost his freedom.

I still think about this amazing young man who still smiled and was happy.

It taught me to look hard and find things for which to be grateful…to be present, accept and find ways to be at peace.

—Sue, an 82-year-young seeker of spiritual wisdom

A HELMET, DRUGS, AND REDEMPTION

In 1985 I was a young motorcycle police officer in a small city—part of a group of fine men and women who loved their work, protected each other and the good people of our city.

I was working solo as a motorcycle traffic officer. I stopped for lunch, parked my bike along the curb, and hung my helmet on the rearview mirror. I glanced back at the bike while I ate lunch. Then I returned to the bike. Confusion! Where was my helmet?

A motorist slowed down, saw my confusion, and said "Some kids in a Camaro stopped by your bike." Now I had the embarrassment of sending out a radio broadcast and riding naked (no helmet) back to the police station.

Over the next few days, I patrolled near local high schools, watching for Camaros. A lucky break came when I stopped a student for speeding and asked about the helmet. Hopeful that I wouldn't ticket him, he admitted who took the helmet.

My riding partner and I shot over to the high school and yanked the student out of class. At the police station for a little "discussion," he surprised us by admitting he'd snatched the helmet to become a campus hero and then had taken it to his uncle's house. Fortunately two detectives recovered the helmet, which was intact. It was embarrassing and humbling, but we got it back.

After retirement, I spent time in community activities and came to know and respect people from all walks of life. One of them, a truly honest and caring man, had spent years riding with an outlaw motorcycle gang. Some of his buddies I knew by name. He was invited to a church, and a transformation began.

One day I was talking with friends about the helmet, and he overhead me and said, "Let me tell you what happened. My nephew brought the helmet to my house so I could trade it for drugs. The detectives came, took the helmet, and left. But I was bummed! It was a cool prize!"

When I asked him if he would have traded the helmet for drugs he said, "absolutely!"

If I had encountered him back then, I would have looked at him with scorn. Today I am less inclined to draw hasty conclusions. I have met people formerly involved with alcohol and drug abuse, and some who had spent time in jail. Now they are living with gratitude and serving others. They are among the finest people I know, and I humbly want to be more like them in their hearts, for God and others.

We can all turn our lives around, make different choices, and join a new "gang."

—*Dave, a happily retired officer, continuing to learn and share*

THE WAKE-UP CALL...
THE CHALLENGES... AND THE GIFTS

I started drinking and using drugs when I was fourteen. I had at least two alcoholic blackouts by the time I was sixteen.

I didn't struggle for survival or experience abuse. My parents were loving and supportive. I went to private schools, and did not want for anything. I had no excuses for my choices, and couldn't blame my family, home life, neighborhood, or schools.

I got a good education and went on to study law. I graduated from law school, got married, and then divorced by the time I took the bar exam.

I failed the exam, took it again and again, and failed again and again. I didn't heed my wake up call, and I continued to be challenged, not only by my addictions, but also by failing the exam so many times—and having failed I my marriage.

Finally I passed the exam and practiced criminal defense law for ten years, from 1980 to 1990. I had started my career but had not overcome my addictions, and kept that part of my life hidden.

During this time I met a wonderful woman, got married, and was also appointed to a County Superior Court Bench. Today my wife and I have been married for thirty-five years.

September 7, 1997, I began my journey to sobriety with support from AA, my sponsor, my wife, my mom, and a wonderful doctor. It was a major decision, and a great opportunity to change a long-standing challenge in my life. And, it is a day-to-day choice.

Today I count my gifts…recovery, life, family, and health. I have a chance to share my experience with others, helping them know that they are not alone.

—*A sober man making a positive difference*

> We can't solve problems by using the same kind of thinking we used when we created them.
> —Albert Einstein

BANANAS

Last week I was surprised when I wept about something that had happened when I was eleven.

In my youth I had many jobs, and one was selling newspapers on a United States Marine Corps base after school. At first I carried a heavy armload of papers through the barracks without much success, because the marines were out working like the civilians. So, my boss told me, "Go to the mess hall and stand at the entrance. The marines will buy them on the way out from dinner." What a relief! I thought I was just a bad salesman or hadn't learned the trick.

One day a pile of boxes full of bananas was on the steps across from me. I stood and watched marines stoop and grab one or two going into the mess hall. All of a sudden I saw the mess sergeant bearing down on me, and I started quaking in my shoes.

I was thinking this was it, and I would get tossed out. This guy was tall, at least 250 pounds, and looked mean as sin. He came up, looked down, and in a deep, gravelly voice said, "Hey kid, if you want some bananas grab them before they're all gone." Then he left, and when my heart slowed down, I took two bananas. I was still employed, had my position at the entrance, and two bananas. Good ... my family needed the money.

So, why some sixty-seven years later did I suddenly weep as I remembered this event? Well, here are some reasons I considered:

* It was one of the first genuinely caring things I had experienced.
* It was a profound event, truly one of joy.

* The mess sergeant metaphorically represented my father, the other sergeant in my life.
* I wish Dad could have shown as much compassion and love.
* I was weeping for my parents, wishing I could talk with them again.
* I was weeping for my youth and the lack of tenderness I'd received.
* Perhaps none of the above, or all of the above.

It remains a mystery, but not an unpleasant one. While confusing, it showed that I have the capacity to be vulnerable and sensitive, and I am not the person I was for a long time.

Throughout our lives we thrive with the compassion, tenderness, and warmth we receive and give.

—Jim, a thoughtful seeker enjoying writing his memoirs and sharing his stories

MY ANGEL FROM HEAVEN

Around the time I turned forty, God decided to bless me, my husband, and our seventeen-year-old daughter, Jasmine, with an angel from heaven. I am referring to our now fifteen-year-old son, Skyler.

Jasmine was excited about having a little brother. Well, when he was born, and unbeknown to her father or me, she was pregnant. Imagine my surprise to find out at forty that I was becoming a mother again, and a grandmother, all at once. The year 2000 was wonderful—full of surprises.

It wasn't until Skyler was three years old that we saw the developmental differences between him and my grandson, Gabriel, who was eleven months younger. We had Skyler tested and found out he was on the autism spectrum. I had grown up with an uncle who had Down syndrome. So, the news didn't throw our family into a tailspin.

We experienced some challenges when Skyler was young. However, my husband and I, along with the whole family, consider ourselves lucky and blessed to have such a loving child in our lives. My son is autistic, and we treat him as we treat others.

Yes, he is in special education at public school, he won't drive a car, and may not get married. He is the person with whom we love to spend time. Simple. Loving. Our angel from heaven!

—Rosemary, 50-something, enjoying life with three generations of family

UNPLANNED NEW LIFE

In 1977 my husband Mo and I, along with our two young children, came to the United States to visit my sister for two months. We arrived with gifts, one suitcase each, and our return tickets back to Iran. I was twenty-two years old.

While we were here we got a telephone call from Mo's mother telling us not to return to Iran. War had broken out, the Shah had been removed from power, and there was a new government. She assured us that the situation was very bad; they were living in the cellar and had no lights after 6 p.m. because of the bombing.

"Please," she said, "stay in America a while longer; it is not safe for you to return." What a dilemma. We had no visas, spoke very little English, and our time to visit was almost over.

So to protect our family we applied for political asylum for the four of us through the American Embassy. We could stay while the applications processed; however, we couldn't work and we were running out of money, so we depended heavily on the hospitality and goodness of my sister.

Finally we received our cards to stay and work. Mo took a job as a busboy in a Persian restaurant, and we both cleaned apartments and offices. We all learned English. The manager of the complex rented us an apartment for only $200, so we could have our own home.

I went to beauty school and got my license as a beautician. Thirty-eight years ago, I began working in the beauty shop at J.C. Penney. We all worked hard to learn and get ahead in our new homeland.

I was lucky. After five years, I was able to buy my own salon in a popular shopping center, where I worked seven days a week, ten hours a day. During that time our daughter assisted, and our son cleaned the shop. Mo also became a hairdresser, but because of a leg problem, he couldn't stand all day, so he began a new career in real estate, where he has been successful.

> *Nothing splendid has ever been achieved except by those who dared believe that something inside of them was superior to circumstance.*
> —Bruce Barton

Today I am a hairdresser working part time, so I can spend time with my dear grandchildren.

As I look back over our lives, who would have imagined starting a whole new life in a different country, with one suitcase, no money, and very little English—far away and out of harm's way?

And here we are today—safe, comfortable, and happy, with successful children and wonderful grandchildren.

My story proves that, with willingness and commitment, we can start over and find our own kind of success and happiness wherever we may land. The United States welcomed us to a new home.

—Sara, 60-year-old, happy and devoted grandmother

CLEAN AND SHINY!

Leo was a precision machinist. He was orderly, meticulous, and thorough, and that included his work in the kitchen. Using several different products and methods, he could scour any pot or pan back to pristine newness, regardless of its prior baking experience.

Once there was a family event after a funeral. As was the Midwestern tradition, the neighbors sent or brought to our home covered dishes such as casseroles or desserts for the visitors. One such contribution, lasagna, came in a much used metal 9 x 12 baking pan.

Eventually Leo returned the pan to its owner. The lady met him at the door of her home, and he handed her the pan.

"Well, that's not mine," she said.

"Umm, well, here is your label on the bottom," Leo said.

He had cleaned the pan beyond her recognition! Now, this was most embarrassing for any traditional housekeeper who believes she has everything always spic and span.

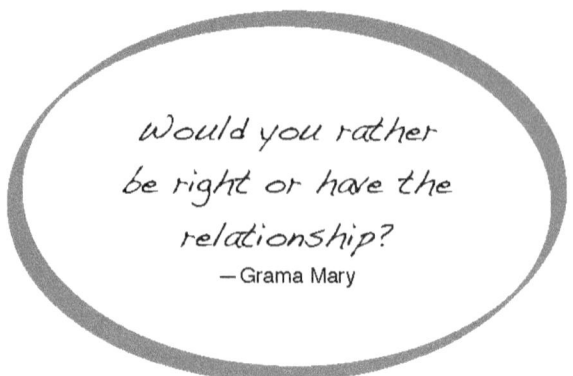

Would you rather be right or have the relationship?
—Grama Mary

Forever after, the running joke among the ladies of the parish was to never send something to Bonnie and Leo's without thoroughly scouring the container beforehand, lest their housekeeping skills be found out.

Well, there are many sides to this story:
* Perhaps it is good to return things as you receive them.
* Or maybe it is best to be a gracious receiver of someone's gift, whatever it might be.
* And it is also possible that wise Leo made sure he didn't have to work so hard in the kitchen, since after that, the ladies in the parish would be bringing their gifts in clean and shiny pans.

Hmm…

—*Bill, 60-something, in memory of Leo, his dear father*

PIES

My dad Leo and his cousin Philip lived across the street from each other while they were growing up. They were the same age and reinforced each other's creative mischief.

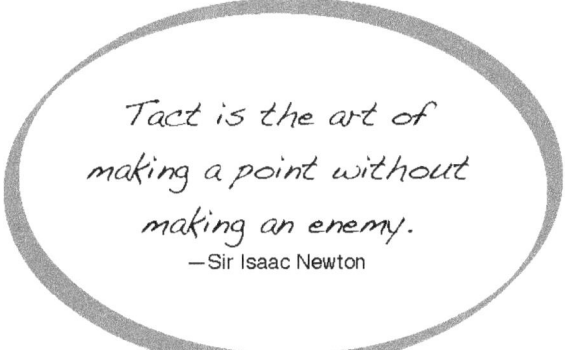

Tact is the art of making a point without making an enemy.
—Sir Isaac Newton

One day they came scrambling into my grandmother Molly's kitchen, where she had just placed a ball of pie dough on the table to roll it out for a pie. Well, cousin Philip lifted his leg, and with the bottom of his shoe smashed the dough ball flat.

One might have expected grandma to become hysterical, trash the dough, or give the boys an earful. No. Without batting an eye, she proceeded to finish rolling out the dough to make the pie.

After all, the boys were the ones who were going to eat it!
Some jokes have two sides.

—Bill, 60-something, IT guy, with stories from the family kitchen

A MIRACLE IN ALASKA

In 1982 I was a pastor in a small city church and was invited by a member to go fishing with him in Alaska. He was raising money for a school in Anchorage.

My way was paid, and my wife said, "Go! It will be a trip of a lifetime." So we flew to Anchorage, met our host who owned the flying service, and spent the night at his lodge.

The next morning we flew in a six-passenger float plane. I was excited looking at the glaciers, moose, deer, and eagles in flight. The wind grew strong as we neared our small lake destination.

It took twenty minutes to get to the dock. The plan was to hike to a nearby river, fish, and float down to another lake.

Change of plans! As it started to rain, a guide said fishing was not good. So, back in the plane and back to our host's lodge. Our plan was to return the next day.

However, as the plane lifted off, it took a sharp left turn, and the left wing dipped into the water. We went into the water backwards, bending and breaking the tail section. Then we were under water with the wings holding us up.

In the plane was the pilot, a doctor friend, my friend Tom, a young teenage guide, and me. Going in backwards broke the back of the seats off, and the cargo doors opened. I climbed out, and my friend Tom came after me. We pulled the boy out and put him on a pontoon. Struggling with my chest waders and boots, I went under water, got one foot out, and came back up. The young boy was gone!

The plane had slipped beneath the water, and everyone was gone except Tom and me. Tom couldn't swim, so I tried to swim to him and the short distance to shore, but the wind was too strong. Tom went under. I had to turn and swim in the other direction, with my waders on one foot, full of water.

I remembered how that summer I had practiced swimming the length of our pool just using my arms—no legs. I was in great physical condition. In that moment, I believe God had guided me to get prepared for this plane crash in the icy Alaska waters.

> *When the wind is knocked out of your sails, there's always an auxiliary motor called faith.*
> — Anonymous

So, I finally made shore. I was wet and cold. Soon, a float plane flew over, I waved but they didn't see me. Later, a large construction helicopter flew over my head. It landed one hundred feet away. Two men jumped out, carried me to the helicopter, wrapped me in warm blankets, and took me to the airport, where I was treated for hypothermia. That evening a military C-130 cargo plane landed, and they invited me to fly to Anchorage with them to catch a flight home.

All the while God was watching over me. It was not my time to go.

—*Tom, enjoying his family and ministry (appeared in* Pentecostal Evangel *7/9/06)*

VALUES SHARED THROUGH GENERATIONS

I am a business coach, and for many years I was a frequent speaker in college business classes.

The students ranged between twenty and twenty-two, and my topic was always about job search and career management.

When I was fresh out of the Army, at the age of twenty-three, I had taken a values assessment and had developed my own abridged version of it. I offered it to students as a way for them to discover their values.

Just before they began, I would quietly write my values down on a piece of paper, fold it, and put it in my pocket. I would say that my values had not really changed since I was their age.

When they finished writing, we would go around the room, so each student could share. No pressure, mind you… this was optional! Of course they wanted to know what I had written, and I would read mine out loud.

It was a sweet moment. Even though I was generations apart from them, we realized that most of our values were the same. So I started to question just how different the generations were when it came to values, and what understanding this could bring.

We are often more alike than we are different.

—Randy, still enjoying teaching, learning, and appreciating common values

HANGING ON THROUGH THE BUMPS OF LIFE

We were traveling on a bumpy, frozen dirt road toward the base of a mountain on a cold November morning just before sunrise. But I was not inside the warm car. I was lying on my stomach on the trunk, desperately trying to hang on.

While I wore gloves, my fingers were freezing as they clung to any small crevice I could dig into. Any moment a bump could rocket me off the car and onto the cold frozen ground. I was miserable, totally miserable. How did I get into this terrible situation?

It was the late sixties in Utah, and I was sixteen, heading out to hunt deer along with some neighbors and Dad in his car. The Utah Fish & Game Department had determined there were too many deer on a mountain close to where we lived. So they opened an extended hunt to reduce the size of the herd. Wolves and mountain lions had kept the deer population in check. However, they were killed off so cattle and sheep could graze in the mountains. We gladly got up at 4 a.m. to be on the mountain before sunrise to hunt the deer for meat.

Part way up the slippery road covered in snow, we got stuck with tires spinning. So Mack and I, the youngest, were told to get out and push the car. They told us that once we got going to jump onto the trunk and hang on, because if they stopped to let us in, the car would get stuck again.

We pushed, got the car going, jumped on the trunk, lay on our stomachs with our feet hanging over the back, and hung on for dear life. And, with each bump in the road, we came closer and closer to being hurled off onto the hard, frozen ground. It seemed that the base of the mountain was light years away.

And, then I heard something completely unexpected. Mack, who looked like a short, tough lumberjack with broad shoulders and a big, bushy moustache, started chuckling. And, with each bump, he would chuckle a deep husky chuckle. First, I thought, *How can he be laughing? Doesn't he see how terrible it is?*

And, then it hit me…how completely absurd our situation was, and that it was actually funny!

So I started to chuckle, too. The bigger the bump and the closer we came to being hurled off the car, the harder we laughed. And then our rollercoaster ride was over. We got off the car and shared a good laugh and immense relief.

So now when life gets bumpy, when it seems like I'm about to eat a mouthful of dirt, I can hear Mack chuckling. And it is good to know that his chuckle will always be there for any, and all crazy rides I may encounter.

—George, 60-something, a happy techie and family man

RICHES MONEY CAN'T BUY

I was born into a humble family living in New England. Mom taught us to have good morals and manners, to be kind and loving, and remember there are two sides to every story.

My dad was promised a job in California, so we packed simple things in our car and headed west. What a long, hot adventure! When we arrived, there was no job, so we lived in a tent, took showers at the park, and worked in prune orchards and canneries. Then we sold the car for a trailer to live in.

Mom worked at OWL Lettershop, which was open late at night and offered services like typing, copying, and printing cards for different clients. All through high school, I worked part time taking inventory for a drug store and helping Mom at OWL. She was a writer who took creative writing classes, and she taught me to write stories.

Love of country, traditions, faith, and forgiveness were important to us through our lives.

I married at nineteen and did a variety of work through my career in both the medical and legal professions, as an office manager, secretary, and legal assistant. My work was varied and rewarding. And, I enjoyed writing, often creating appreciation speeches. My husband and I are now celebrating our fifty-ninth anniversary.

The riches that money can't buy are the values of kindness, charm, appreciation, and good manners—things that humble beginnings can teach us.

—Joyce, 78, still appreciating the good in people

SISTER JUNE…THE ENTREPRENEUR

In the 1960s I was teaching in a private catholic grammar school. In the evenings older students took catholic instruction, and a student left behind a book about handwriting analysis. I picked it up, became fascinated, and started looking for resources.

I found a correspondence school in Chicago that offered courses in Graphoanalysis, and signed up. After two years, I was certified as a graphoanalyst and began researching European graphology through books I ordered and borrowed. This was a wonderful way to help individuals and businesses hiring people.

While I was still teaching, I began a business in handwriting analysis. I was one of several people quoted in an article in *USA Today*. A CEO called, wondering how I could offer an analysis of a whole personality from one page. Of course he wanted his analysis done first! He remained a client for over twenty years and introduced me to other CEOs, including two CEOs of casinos.

I was now an entrepreneur, and this income went to the head of my order, paid bills, and supported our other charitable work.

I began teaching graphology, and from an ad twenty to fifty students would sign up. I worked with men, women, and children, and visited almost every state teaching other analysts. And I lectured on ships…I was the teacher with a cross hanging from her neck!

In the 1970s, Sister Harriet, a great writer teaching at the university, took my course. "Let's write our own correspondence course," she said, and we began putting our work on tapes.

I stopped teaching school because I saw clients every day, managed the correspondence course, and was out lecturing. We wanted to help people beyond our church work. And in the eighties I found Father Wirling's lectures about temperaments. Sister Harriet then wrote a book called, *Your Temperaments are Showing,*

In 1984 we formed our own publishing company, Insyte Inc. I sold the correspondence course and continued my work from the nineties until 2012. And in 2013, I retired and sold the business to another analyst. I still do some one-page analyses from time to time.

People like me don't really retire.

—Sister June, 85, who has made such a difference through her service as a nun, entrepreneur, and graphologist

STICKS!

When my brothers, Ben and Mike, and I were in our teens, our Dad said he had something to say and asked us to sit down near his workshop.

Well, we sat on a five-gallon bucket, an old tire, and a pile of wood. He asked us to go to the backyard hillside, find a stick, and come back. With puzzled looks we did as we were asked, and returned, each with a stick in hand.

As we sat down again he asked us to break our sticks. Again with puzzled looks, we did so with ease. *Snap, Snap, Snap!* "Now," he said, "go and gather a big bundle of sticks and return." And, so we did.

As we sat there wondering what crazy idea he had, he asked us to try to break our bundles of sticks. We couldn't even snap a one. Dad smiled and said, "Boys, these bundles of sticks represent family and strength. Alone you can be broken, but with family together, you can never be broken, just like the bundle of sticks."

Dad's way of teaching this lesson lives on in each of us. Through the years, all six siblings have had ups and downs, helped each other, and stayed close—like the bundle of sticks.

I have shared that story with many families. And there is a reminder above my garage door—a bundle of sticks.

—Pat, 66, Reiki master and music lover

TEACHING AND LEARNING IN THE PEACE CORP

In 1960 President Kennedy announced a plan to send Americans overseas to encourage understanding between the U.S. and other nations. It was called the Peace Corp, and I was hooked. So in 1964 after college I applied and was accepted into a group going to the Philippines.

We trained in Hilo Hawaii with Filipino teachers, studying their language and culture. Because there are more than one hundred different languages and dialects, we were in three groups, each learning the language of our assigned region. I was taught Ilocano, the language of northern Luzon. My mentor was a high school math teacher.

After training we enjoyed a short vacation before boarding the plane for Manila to begin the next two years of our lives. My assignment was teaching math at La Union High School in San Fernando in Luzon.

Since the Philippines had been under U.S. rule, their educational system was based on ours. I taught basic algebra and trigonometry, and soon became a true part of the faculty. And in my second year, I also began teaching at a Catholic high school, where each day we began by singing the Lord's Prayer. Being Jewish, I had never learned it.

The people of San Fernando were warm and welcoming, and when a local group put on a play, I learned an Ilocano song. After twenty-five years, I still remember the melody and words.

I extended my tour through the second summer. Another teacher and I set up a summer camp. In the mornings, high school students helped elementary students, and in the afternoons, they played games, went on fieldtrips, and rehearsed a play. A U.S. charity sent dry milk to the Catholic church, and since it wasn't used, I arranged to get it to the local ice cream company. We enjoyed ice cream every day.

It was not easy to leave San Fernando, where I had been welcomed. Even now, remembering all those kindnesses brings warmth to my heart. Often when I meet Filipinos I ask if they are from northern Luzon and speak Ilocano. When they say yes I invite them to sing "Dung, dung wen canto" with me.

> *What the heart gives away is never gone ... It is kept in the hearts of others.*
> — Robin St. John

Recently, while volunteering at Kaiser Hospital, a woman said that when she'd left the hospital with her new baby I had sung a Filipino lullaby for them, so we sang it again. For her, it was the gift of Filipino memories, and for me, it was a way to hold onto memories of the time I'd spent in the Peace Corp in the Philippines.

Our memories of times shared with others become the treasures of our lives. And meeting people from remembered times and places is priceless. It is indeed a very small world!

—*Laurie, enjoying her life and her wonderful memories*

THE GOLD KEY AND THE SILVER KEY

After I had a modern dance and choreography career, a position in a traditional southern Filipino Kulintang music and dance company, and a stint at performance art, a friend asked me, "Do you tell stories? I want one for a conference I'm producing." My co-director Robert and I looked at each other, knowing we didn't tell stories. We smiled, nodded, and said, "Yes." It was a paid gig! And, we soon found the ancient Chinese tale, "Ten Thousand Treasure Cave."

> *A farming couple, because of their generosity, were given two keys to the Ten Thousand Treasure Cave: a gold key to enter the cave of infinite treasures, any of which was theirs for the taking, and a silver key to leave. They were warned to never forget the silver key.*
>
> *Instead of jewels, gold, or silver they chose three simple farm tools. When they returned home, they found the tools were magic....making enough rice, wheat, and corn to feed the villagers. When the Emperor heard about the magic, he demanded the tools for himself. But, when he tried to use them, they produced ash.*
>
> *"Lead me to this cave immediately! What? A gold key?" and the greedy Emperor grabbed the gold key before the farmer could explain about the silver key. Into the cave the Emperor and his troops stormed. Slam! went the cave door.*

Bedazzled by all the sparkling jewels, they soon discovered there was no way out.

Having never seen a storyteller before, we put this story together combining our tools…theatre experience, dance, and music. Asian tellers were scarce, and soon we were asked to perform at the National Storytelling Festival. Very quickly our storytelling style launched a national dialogue across the country. People said we moved too much, used phony costumes, and didn't use real Asian words.

There are many ways cultures tell stories—Hawaiians with dancing and graceful hands, East Indians with gestures, facial expressions and rhythm, Chinese with a musician, and Japanese seated at a low table, using a fan as a prop. There is not just one way to tell a story.

We did not change our storytelling style to suit the little emperors. Our tools became our treasures, weaving movement, music, and the spoken word. We told pan-Asian tales that connected their inherent values to today's issues. Others thanked us for giving them the courage to add movement to their telling. We began to tour around the world.

Our treasured tools continue to delight audiences. We discovered our mission…to build cultural bridges that celebrate diversity and create compassionate communities through stories revealing universal truths. Random situations happen; use them as opportunities.

You never know when someone hands you a golden key. Will you use it for community, or find yourself in a cave with no silver key?

—Nancy and Robert of Eth-Noh-Tec, enchanting many with music, dance and storytelling

ROCKS, STONES, BRICKS…AND PEOPLE

I am standing in my yard surrounded by piles of stones, bricks, and boulders, and in my head I see a vision of a stone wall that has been a lifetime in the making. My eyes have always been attracted to stones. I've collected them on childhood camping adventures, throughout my adolescent summers, and during road trips through the west with my good friend, Bruce. I found many near rivers and on beaches—stones softly shaped by time and water.

> *The foundation stones for a balanced success are honesty, character, integrity, faith, love, and loyalty*
> —Zig Ziglar

I love walls designed in the craftsman tradition of the early 1900s—a random mix of vintage brick and water-washed boulders. Retirement allows me to build my wall without the constraints of time and attention.

I approach the design with a vision, as each stone is unique in its size, shape, and appearance. I have learned to respect each one for its own unique journey—shaped by water flowing over it for countless hundreds of years and moved by forces it could never control.

Building with stones is a creative process, one of patience and attention. Stones are held, flipped, and turned countless times until their placement, which is determined by the stones around them. Each placement decides the appearance and place of the next.

There are no instructions, and I have discovered that it cannot be forced. I have spent many hours trying to make a stone fit a location, only to succumb and abandon my initial plan.

And, my patience is always rewarded with a visual accomplishment reflecting that effort.

As in any creative human process—whether loving your partner, raising a child, or building a stone wall—the eye recognizes care, respect, and passion.

And, isn't this a metaphor…each of us is unique in our size, shape and appearance, with our own journeys and ways to fit with others.

—Steve, happily retired husband and father, designing and building his unique rock wall

IT'S THE INNER BEAUTY THAT COUNTS

In high school my friend Sue was a model, and she had all kinds of titles, including "Miss Dixie Cup." Well, I was pleased to be seen with "Miss Dixie Cup."

We were going to a Friday night basketball game to watch her boyfriend, Mike, play. He had flaming red hair and freckles, and they were going steady.

Sue wore a beautiful blue angora sweater, a string of shiny pearls, and her freshly polished saddle shoes. She had soft dark curls, long dark eyelashes, and wore wonderful perfume. This was going to be fun.

We got to the gym early to get good seats so Sue could yell encouraging words to Mike. This was an important game in the finals. Mike played well in the first quarters, and Sue was thrilled. The scores were close, and Mike shot a basket and broke the tie.

Sue stood up and cheered loudly, but suddenly people were giggling. Mike had thrown the ball in the wrong basket, and the coach took him out of the game. The crowd applauded him for his efforts as he turned as red as his hair.

Sue was furious and yelled, "How could you be so stupid and embarrass me?" It wasn't fun being with her the rest of the game.

I looked at Sue in a different way after that, and I thought to myself, *Maybe it is the inner beauty that really counts.*

—Anonymous wiser woman who appreciates inner beauty

THREE GOALS I SET...AND MET

I was born in Chicago one of two daughters in a Polish Italian family. When I was eight, Mom and Dad separated, and we lived with Dad and visited Mom on weekends. Usually we went to movies, where there was little quality time together. When I was sixteen, Dad remarried, and I did not have an easy relationship with my stepmother. Often I would sit in the attic reading books, imagining myself in the stories.

After high school, I attended junior college in the evenings and studied psychology and English. I also had a variety of little jobs. There I was, a young woman who had never been downtown or danced with a boy.

This is where the story begins. I set three goals for myself...to see the world, be a young mother and grandmother, and be president of a corporation. It was time to get started!

A cousin invited me to a wedding in a downtown hotel. It was an excuse to go upstairs to a singles dance...so off we went. A tall, good-looking, blue-eyed boy asked me to dance. Suddenly I realized my cousin had left, and I didn't know how to get home. So I crowded into a small coupe car with this man and his buddies, who were all over six-feet tall, and they drove me home.

Well, for some time I went out with him and his group, and the following spring we got married, and later had three children. During my lifetime I often turned the other cheek, choosing my battles. After twenty-two years of married life, when my son was eleven and my daughters were seventeen and twenty, we divorced. I was forty-four and ready to continue the life of my dreams. Finances were tight, and my mother was a big help.

The following year I decided I was strong and started a travel business with a partner. We were together for two years, and then I was on my own, starting all over. I used to say I was married to my business and had weekend husbands! After six years, I incorporated and became the company president. I loved motivating the ten great women working for us. And for the next twenty years, I traveled all over the world.

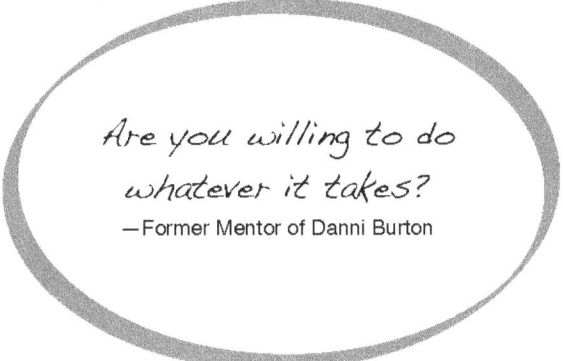
Are you willing to do whatever it takes?
—Former Mentor of Danni Burton

In 1982 I became a grandmother at fifty-five. In 1988 I sold the business to an outside buyer for a quarter of a million dollars. I had achieved the three goals that I'd set for myself! I was very comfortable in my life, but I was bored, so with the help of a young protégé, I began an Italian import business. The vendors are small or family-owned businesses. Our motto is… "You treat us right, and we will treat you right." I am still going strong!

So, I encourage others to keep dreaming, look for new adventures, and stay positive.

—*Lee Marie, an amazing entrepreneur*

A SIMPLE PHRASE...WELCOME HOME

I was born in Wyoming, and when I was a baby my dad left, and Mom didn't have work, so she put me in an orphanage until she remarried a man in the Air Force. They had a son and daughter, and his career brought all of us out to California.

My stepfather beat my mom and all of us, and at thirteen, I began running away from home. I ended up in juvenile hall for stealing Mom's car. Finally at fifteen I jumped on two freight trains and hitchhiked to a friend's home, and his parents adopted me. I started high school, worked in the car wash, and had a girlfriend. I was safe and happy.

At eighteen I got drafted into the Army and was stationed in Germany as a truck mechanic on wheel vehicles and tanks. I reenlisted for aviation school as a mechanic working on turbine motors in helicopters.

I got married while I was in the Army, but sadly that didn't work out. Worse, I got busted for drugs and spent three months in the stockade. However, I did get an honorable discharge at age twenty-three. FMC company was hiring mechanics, so I got a job and married again.

I wanted a motorcycle, but I couldn't get a loan, so I decided to build one. Every week I took money from my check to buy a part for the bike. In 1973 it was finished. I left my wife and my job and started hanging out with bikers.

I was drinking, using drugs, and picking up girls in bars. It was party, party. While I had temporary courage with drugs, the highs weren't worth the lows. So, I stopped riding my bike.

In the eighties I became the lease owner of an auto glass shop. I worked there and lived in the back. I started thinking that my life was over. I drank whiskey and antifreeze, lay down, and seven days later I woke up in the hospital. I had been in a coma, had seizures, and couldn't believe I'd survived. The county psych ward cared for me, and then I went back to the shop.

During this time, a wonderful woman pursued me. She was my rock, and we stayed together for twenty-two years until her passing.

In spite of detoxing at the VA Hospital and going to AA, I began drinking again. Here I was just two blocks from the police station in my auto glass shop servicing police cars. I tried to get sober. And, then a friend invited me to a meeting at a local church. I cried when I saw a brochure that said "Welcome Home."

Today I am six years clean and sober. I have stopped smoking, and I now sublease the shop. I live modestly in an apartment with my granddaughter and her family. There are still challenges to overcome. I do it one day at a time.

— *Dave, 68, finally finding his home*

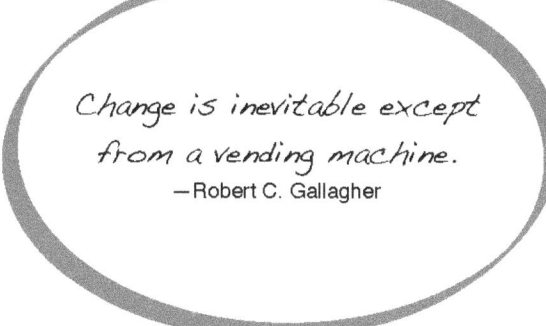

WHEN IN DOUBT... STICK TOGETHER

In a way this story is a metaphor for life.

In 2007 our family was traveling in Europe. At the time, our daughter was sixteen and our son was thirteen. We stood near our luggage and looked for the train or shuttle to take us to the airport. My wife, the organizer, held our passports and tickets.

Well, my wife, with two suitcases, got on a shuttle, and I was standing on the platform with two teenagers and the rest of the luggage. Somehow we got on the wrong shuttle and ended up at the wrong terminal.

Had my wife and two suitcases managed to get to the right terminal? So we had to get off, luggage and all, and head back on another shuttle. We finally arrived at the right terminal.

What a mix up, and what a lesson.

So, like it is in life…when in doubt stick together whether you are a family, a team of athletes, travelers, rescuers, business professionals, or your "village."

—Bruce, who knows the importance of team spirit

SIXTY AND JUST GETTING STARTED!

When my dad was my age, he started a business that he sold twenty-five years later at age eighty-seven for ten million dollars. He was a forward-thinking and ahead-of-his-time guy. I vowed to be like him…a late bloomer, starting at an age when others are packing their tents and heading home.

Now I am at that magical and significant age, anticipating the next thirty years with gusto and excitement. Retiring at age sixty-five is an old and popular notion, when that was close to the average lifespan. Today, living to one hundred and beyond is common. Instead of dying in our sixties, many of us feel more alive than ever in our golden years.

As this year moved toward me, I spoke about my impending success, thinking I was about to walk in my dad's footsteps. However, I discovered that I had unwittingly bought into some cultural projections about age, which I recognized as uncomfortable and self-limiting thoughts floating inside of my head.

So I decided what I wanted to think, and what expectations I wanted to live. I traded in cultural limitations for my own nourished and cultivated belief that I may just be getting started! What happened next was miraculous, and a shift occurred inside me.

Doors have been flying open. Educational opportunities have presented themselves, and I have the curiosity of a college student who is eager to learn. My energy, excitement, and enthusiasm for the next phase of my wellness business is more focused than ever. A curtain has been lifted—the last vestige between me, my future, and what is possible.

My dad had very poor health. As a Holistic Health Coach, I have made different choices. I lead by example, inspiring clients to steer in a much happier direction. Thankfully, I am in excellent health.

My dad was my hero, and he prospered despite his health challenges. With my portal open and intentions clear, my dreams are moving toward me as I move toward them. With the drive I inherited from him, and my commitment to my health priority, I have a powerful combination for which I feel such gratitude.

> *Behind every great daughter is a truly amazing dad.*
> —Anonymous

I no longer think of retirement or have any thoughts about stopping my meaningful work as a health coach and businesswoman. I understand dad's excitement. I wish to continue blessing people's lives, and being rewarded financially for my efforts and abilities. I want to pay it forward by inspiring others to open their portals.

Let's remember that there is no tent to pack up—only a life full of ongoing exploration of each new year's possibilities.

—*Rosie, working, playing, and living life to the fullest*

DO YOUR HOMEWORK AND BE PREPARED

I was born into a lower middle class family in India, and I aspired to be a doctor. My father supported me on a meager income, and my completing medical school was a sacrifice for him. My family was very supportive of my education and career.

After graduation I joined government service working as a junior physician in a small, rural town, while I still dreamed of studying abroad. In time I married and had a child.

Destiny compelled me to take the qualifying exam for internship and residency training in the U.S. I passed the test and received letters from several hospitals.

One medical center in Buffalo, New York, invited me to join its program. I responded that I was interested but financially unable to travel. So, the hospital sent tickets for the three of us with the intention of recovering the travel expenses from my salary.

Suddenly, we were on our way to a new life in a new country. And, we had not done our homework! So, we arrived in December in freezing snow and ice, but dressed for India weather. We had no winter coats, boots, or hats.

So while it is good to remember that when it is your destiny, the universe will move you, it is also good to do your homework and be prepared!

—*Venugopal 79, and Madavi 74, happily retired in California*

CARING AND BEING CARED FOR

My husband and I lived in a beautiful community near the ocean, and every other week after church, I drove four hours to my daughter's home to babysit. I would stay for three days, and then drive the four hours back home.

During one stay my son had arranged to buy a new car, and I offered to take him to pick it up. While waiting in the truck, I suffered a stroke and was taken to a nearby hospital.

I spent three weeks in Kaiser Hospital, and then transferred to an acute rehab hospital for four weeks. My left side was paralyzed, and I just wanted to go home. One morning the occupational therapist helping me dress saw that both of my legs were in one hole of my Winnie-the-Pooh boxer shorts. We laughed when she said I had my knickers in a twist!

So I was released, rented a wheelchair, and went back home. A friend and my husband got me into the house, up to the bedroom, and into bed.

My daughter had two children and was expecting her third. Her son used to put his hand on her tummy and sing "Twinkle, Twinkle Little Star" to the baby. When the baby was due, we drove the four hours to the hospital to meet our newest grandchild. My grandson was leaning into the bassinet telling the baby, "Sometimes I will call you crackers, because I love you, and love them, too."

Eleven years later, my husband fell off a ladder, and broke several ribs, which exacerbated his oncoming dementia. And then he was diagnosed with Alzheimer's disease. I kept praying for God to handle all these challenges. They were all too big for me.

During this time my daughter looked for an assisted living and memory care community near them. She found a two-bedroom apartment that was available and put a deposit on it for us. Then we went to look at the apartment. And, as we came through the front door, I thought, "I am home."

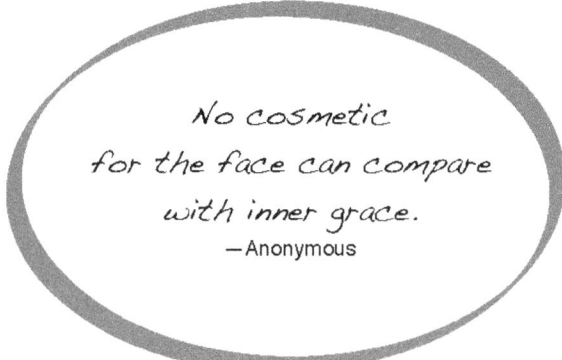

No cosmetic for the face can compare with inner grace.
—Anonymous

We have settled in and made this our new home. I do believe that God brought us here. I have made peace with being in a wheelchair and missing the connection with my husband.

Sometimes he tells me I am his pretend wife. I reply that I would not pretend to be anyone's wife for thirty years! Thank goodness for my two children and three grandchildren who bring me joy and fun.

Never start or end your day without being grateful for your blessings.

—*Cathy, age 66, residing with dignity in her new community*

GRANDMA ROSE

Our family came to the United States from Italy, and became ranchers in the Santa Clara valley.

Rose had only a grade eight education, and out of necessity, as the older child, she dropped out of school. She worked around the house helping with her younger siblings.

Even without much education, she was very smart and a great storyteller. I loved being with her, and she made a great impact on my life. At fifteen she taught me to drive, and she was always my loving mentor.

In 1972, when she was in her early fifties, she beat breast cancer. In the 1980s, she beat it again. She would say, "Don't worry about me; I have got this. If you worry you don't get past your fears."

From this wonderful woman I learned persistence, compassion, and a desire to better myself. I still remember how she taught me to be strong and push through whatever challenged me.

I have thanked this sweet woman so many times for being such a mentor, inspiration, and guide in my life. Today I am a better man because of knowing her wit and wisdom.

—Joe, 50-something, an advocate for justice and community service

A SIMPLE SCOTTISH STORY

I was raised in the beautiful city of Edinburgh, Scotland, famous for many things, including its castle. Life was school, chores, sports, and lots of Scottish music. We Scots are a practical lot who enjoy humor, music, and stories, which helped during and after the war.

In 1945 I was called up for service in the British Army, serving in the Royal Signals. In 1947 I spent time in Singapore, my first adventure away from Great Britain.

Back to Edinburgh, and working with the Telephone Exchange. I enjoyed marching with the Edinburgh pipe band, proudly wearing my Hunting Stewart kilt. What's a Scotsman without a kilt?

My sister Kitty married an American engineer and moved to California. So, Mom, Dad, and I came for a holiday. They suggested that I get a permanent work visa. So, I worked as an electronics technician, took night classes at USF, and received a BA in English literature, balancing the math in my life.

I was a British subject living in San Francisco, enjoying hiking, Scottish dancing, and working in the communications and power industries as an electronics technician.

KILT —
it's what happened
to the last person who
called it a skirt.
—Unknown

I began to experience arthritis, which limited my mobility. Kitty found me a wonderful apartment in this retirement community, where I am enjoying my life. And, I get around with my walker and wheelchair just fine.

I still sing the Scottish hiking song at full volume!

—An 88-year-young content Scotsman in California

WHAT I TEACH AND WHAT I LEARN

Betty is an energetic and warm ninety-one-year-old lady living in a small city in Ontario, Canada.

She is modest, and doesn't realize how much she has inspired women for more than seventy years.

She still drives, teaches Sunday school, and has started a women's group, ages twenty to ninety. How she brings three or four generations together to talk and share is worthy of admiration.

All she says is, "We ninety year olds are learning a lot about what it is like to be in this high-tech and fast-moving world as a twenty something. And, they are amazed that we managed to get through school, have careers, get married, have children, buy homes, and retire…without a computer, cellphone or iPad."

She loves to teach, is still a curious learner, and has a positive view of life. Has hardship, loss, or struggle visited her? Today she is a widow, has supported addictive struggles within her family, and comforted others through shared loss. What is her secret—if she has one? She quietly claims her faith and deep spiritual convictions.

If you go to visit her, you will get a real cup of tea out of a teapot under a handmade cozy. And, if you look out the window, you could see clothes blowing and drying on a line.

—Danni, one of Betty's former Sunday School students

DON'T PUT ALL YOUR APPLES IN ONE BASKET

I was a young, single woman living in Mumbai, India. Three of my friends and I decided to have a train holiday in Italy. So we flew to Rome and boarded a train to Pompei.

We decided to pool our resources and keep all our money and passports together in my bag.

We were busy having fun, and suddenly the train stopped. I put my head out and realized we were at the Pompei station but several compartments back from the platform. We all ran forward through the compartments to get off on the platform.

Don't sweat the small stuff.
—Richard Carlson

One of my friends and I got off, but the train started off with our other friends still onboard! So there we were, frantically waving at each other and realizing I had all the passports and money in my bag.

We ran to the stationmaster, who spoke only Italian, and all of us began gesturing and talking in different languages. We began praying for help. This was 1982, long before cellphones.

Somehow, our friends got off at the next station and asked that excited stationmaster to call our stationmaster in Pompei. Arrangements were made. They returned on the next train, and from then on we each kept our own passports and money throughout the rest of the trip.

I do believe those prayers had a lot of power. Like the apples in the basket, don't hoard your love, kindness or generosity…spread them around.

—*Kamal, 64, enjoying her life*

BURYING THE HATCHET

"Things are not as they seem. Nor are they otherwise."

I have no idea who said this—my preacher or the local drug store guy. No matter who said it, I have experienced it many times.

My aunt Annie died last week at ninety-nine, and she carried a lot of grudges to her grave. Grandfather provided plots for all nine children, but Annie did not want to be buried next to her sister Opal. She will be buried in a different spot.

I have written stories about my dysfunctional family, but it goes beyond them. I wonder what made me different. What saved me from the destruction of grudge-bearing?

Early on I realized that I could hurt, suffer, or complain…or I could play or see something else. I learned that, instead of being revengeful, I could help other people. Instead of covering my head and sobbing, I could be mesmerized with life and learn to savor the moments.

Reading was part of my salvation, and often I had only the book and the space I was reading in. I would sprawl in my space, hold the book, and listen to the whisper of the pages as I turned them one-by-one. My heart would open in slow motion, old grudges would vanish, and grievances would shrink to manageable sizes. I saw people for who they were.

I realized that all humans want and need exactly the same things: to feel safe, to belong, to be loved, and to be respected. It is so simple, and yet being human can be challenging.

What does it cost us to hold on to grudges? And what do we gain when we bury the hatchet?

Such an old fashioned expression—burying the hatchet. It simply means ending the grudge.

> *Forgiveness is the fragrance that the violet sheds on the heel that has crushed it.*
> —Mark Twain

    Acknowledging our infiniteness is what gives us connectedness with others. All I have to do is let God enter my life and be my track coach. And I pray not for things I want, but for being changed in ways I can't come close to imagining.

    It is a prayer I need to remember everyday.

—Chuck, 83, enjoying writing and sharing stories with his memoirs class

THE COMPASS THAT GUIDES US

I was born and raised on a small dairy farm along the Fox River in Wisconsin. My grandfather and great uncles cleared the land and built the farm after emigrating from Prussia (Germany) in 1856.

My siblings and I attended all eight years of grade school in the same one-room schoolhouse with the same teacher. The eight grades usually totaled thirty-eight students. It was in this environment that I formed my moral and ethical foundation with my informal education in personal responsibility and economy.

I was raised to be frugal and, sixty years later, was amazed to discover that this is how I had lived my life.

"Use it up, wear it out, make it do, or do without."

People have referred to that saying as the Yankee Creed.

I was drafted into the army in 1965, came to Fort Ord, California, and during this time married and began a family. While pursuing satisfying work in the financial industry, I did not seem to have a plan for advancing my career. We often discover, as we move through life, that there is no blueprint. Or, if there is one, it is impossible to follow.

I experienced a turning point in the early 1990s. I survived an employment merger and acquisition and a divorce from my wife. However, those years taught me that a compass had been guiding me. Whether I credit that to my rural upbringing or the spirituality that overtook me through these challenges, I now understand that Someone was watching over me all this time.

After working in a successful career and being happily remarried, I have found there is no joy like giving back. You may find me today volunteering in several ministries at church, with Cancer CAREpoint, and as a docent at Martial Cottle Agpark.

My wife says that my theme song is "Call Me Irresponsible." But then is there not a fair portion of irony in life?

By giving from wherever we are, with whatever we have, we can make a difference in the world.

—Dave, happy husband, father, and grandfather

THE MAGIC OF BOOKS

As a little girl growing up in Birmingham, England, I remember hearing the sound of stray bombs and air raid sirens during WWII. We had few clothes or toys, limited food, and no libraries, and my few books were classics given to me.

My father was a pharmacist, and he watched for fires, so we didn't see much of him. I loved having Mom read to me. In 1942 I started school and was thrilled because there were books with lots of stories. I was a good student, got top grades, and was inspired by reading.

From 1946 on, we often went to visit my aunt and uncle in London, which was 120 miles away by train. They had such a wonderful collection of books...mysteries, thrillers, biographies, and classics. Since I didn't have any playmates, I would pore through the books and magazines.

At age eleven I took an exam, and was entered into high school from age eleven to seventeen. I then spent one year in secretarial training at a community college. I got a job as a secretary and typist, joined a book club, met my husband in a church group, and got married.

In 1966, with two boys under the age of two, we came to America for my husband's job, and I often took my toddlers to the library. I wanted to make sure they had plenty of books.

There I was in a new country, away from all that was familiar and remembered.

Our Peruvian neighbors loved music, and one played a Recorder, so my husband bought me a Recorder, and I joined the Mid-Peninsula Recorder Orchestra. I was enjoying my love of books *and* music.

My husband left when the boys were teenagers. I volunteered at the high school, and then asked for a job, beginning in one department and then moving to the library. During this time, I completed a two-year degree as a Library Technician. Oh, how I loved books!

I go back to England to visit my aunt, who is now 102. She is also blind and somewhat deaf. She will ask me what I am reading. She says, "It's not the same as having someone read it to you as reading for yourself." The person doesn't portray the story as you imagine it.

Whenever a friend is down I send a "thought for the day." I do believe that books have been a constant source of comfort for me throughout my life.

—Jean, retired and joyfully reading and sharing music and gardening

TURNING DIRTY INTO $$$$

I was born and raised in Taiwan, where there are lots of people, noise, and activity. I finished school in Taiwan, and wanted to get my degree in business administration. So I came to the U.S. and enrolled at Mary Hardin College in Texas. What a culture shock!

A friend came and joined me, and in 1970 we moved to New York City, where I was the assistant controller for Miles Metal in Manhattan for seven years. My friends from Taiwan and I decided to come together in California, become partners, and buy a four-plex. Living in one unit and having rental income was a good investment at that time.

I took a position as assistant controller, and then was promoted to controller at San Jose Steel Company, where I worked for seven years before the company closed.

During this time I wanted to improve my management skills. So I got my MBA degree through the University of Phoenix.

However, the entrepreneur in me wanted my own business. So, at a trade show I saw a sign in a booth that said "Turn dirty into big $$$$." I bought a franchise with Dry Clean USA. Now I was the manager, and training at fifteen other stores. In 1993 Dry Clean USA moved out of California, and I began my business called Dry Clean Pro.

My mother kept asking me, "With all your education, why do you want to be a cleaner?"

My answer was, "I invested in my own business, and I enjoy managing, training, and meeting people. Someone else is working on the clothes!"

Twenty-seven years ago I joined the Cupertino Chamber of Commerce. I wanted to understand the American business culture. Through the Asian American Business Council and the Mandarin Business Seminars, I mentor Asian people starting businesses. Twice a year I present a seminar for Asian people throughout the Bay area.

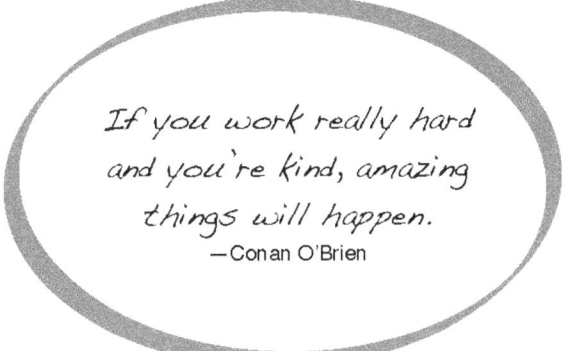

If you work really hard and you're kind, amazing things will happen.
—Conan O'Brien

The Chamber of Commerce honored me with the Star Award and Bridge Award. The city of Cupertino presented me with the Crest Award. I received the Small Business Award of the Year from assemblyman Paul Fong with the State of California. It is so rewarding to be honored for community service, good business practices, and achievements.

When you have been successful, it is important to turn and assist others with your time and knowledge, supporting them to also succeed.

—Vicky, 70, happy entrepreneur, community leader and dry cleaning expert

CARING BEYOND OUR DUTY

This is a story of caring above and beyond duty in a small city police department.

I had been a detective for about six years specializing in robberies and homicides with a small city police department. Sadly, we see a lot of things that can harden your heart and make you wonder about the goodness of people. And most people we meet have formed their own opinions about any and all police officers.

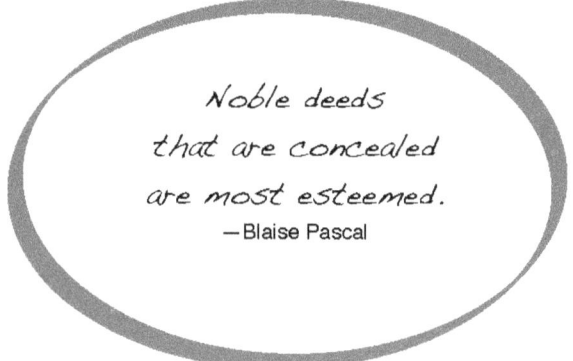

Noble deeds that are concealed are most esteemed.
—Blaise Pascal

One day we got a call about a robbery of a dear lady in her late seventies who lived in a senior retirement apartment complex nearby. Her caregiver and a friend came into her apartment, put a bag over her head, and put a gun to her temple. They shut off her oxygen, stole her last $600 intended for her rent and all her costume jewelry, and fled.

She managed to call us, and we responded. We made sure her oxygen was back on and immediately began our investigation. However, we decided this was not enough. There was a human side here.

We took up a collection at the police station, raised $800, came back with the money, and changed her locks on the door. She was so relieved and so touched by our gesture.

Treating one of our seniors in such a way was unforgivable. We found the caregiver, who was on probation for fraud and forgery. She wanted the money for her son who was in prison. We also found most of her precious jewelry and were happy to return it to this dear lady.

These are the kinds of goodwill and caring gestures that happen without being advertised.

So, the next time you see police officers at the coffee shop, consider they may have had caring moments beyond their duties.

We always appreciate a smile.

—Anonymous detective in a small city somewhere

THE VILLAGE RAISED THE CHILD

My parents and older sister were born in Mexico. In the 1950s they emigrated to Chicago, where I was born. My father left when I was seven and turned our family upside down. Unfortunately after he left, we lived in impoverished neighborhoods called "melting pots."

My Spanish-speaking mother had to get a job, and because she didn't speak English, she worked in factories. A determined woman, she attended night school, learned English and typing, and got a day job and later a swing shift job at the bank. My older sister took care of us. At age ten, I got a job going door to door selling newspaper subscriptions. You needed to be eleven, so I said I was. I wanted to help the family.

Summers were so hot, and we had no air conditioning or car. Winters were so cold our faces burned from the frigid air. The neighborhood was infested with gangs and addicts. Once an older boy beat me, and I ended up in the hospital with a head injury. A group of kids robbed me on the way to school; they threw bricks at my brother and me. And our bedroom was burglarized.

We survived because my mother was strong and instilled in us a sense of purpose. She said, "Do well in school, and become a doctor, lawyer, or engineer, and help others."

Each day I went school, worked until early evening, and stayed out of trouble. I played softball with friends who were in gangs, but they didn't bother me because I was a good player.

I succeeded because of that cliché that it takes a village to raise a child. Teachers recommended me for city-run programs. I had the opportunity to visit the zoo and attend a summer camp. Our group went to Washington, D.C., and saw many of the historical monuments and museums.

My teachers recommended I go to a Jesuit high school. I took the test and received a four-year scholarship that covered tuition. We had to finance getting me to school, which was an hour away. In my junior year, I was one of twenty students selected to go to Peru for seven weeks to build schools in remote villages in the Andes mountains.

I was no angel. In that environment you do things to survive. I finished high school and went to college, but I wasn't motivated. So, after freshman year, I left, joined the Navy, and got to see parts of Asia, Australia, and Africa. I returned, moved to California, went back to college, graduated, and went on to law school.

Today I help poor people who are in trouble with the law. I understand them. For many of them, it takes a village to get them past their addictions.

Now I am one of the villagers offering support, just as I was supported.

—Enrique, dedicated attorney, proud husband, and father of two

HOW I NOW INSPIRE...
AS I WAS INSPIRED

I grew up in Wyoming in a Japanese American family. We were the only minorities in town, and I felt different from other children. My father inspired me. He was a veterinarian with a good reputation, who made his living helping the farmers in our area. My mom learned to adopt and belong by joining social clubs and doing service in the community.

My fourth grade teacher took an interest in me and helped me realize that I was the same as everyone else. What a blessing at that time in my young life.

> *The best teachers are those who show you where to look, but don't tell you what to see.*
> — Alexandra K. Trenfor

I grew up, went to school, and became a high level executive...very much a Type A personality.

And then I had a wake-up call at fifty-five when I was involved in a serious car accident. I suffered a broken neck, broken hip, and shattered elbow and ankle.

After surgery I remained in physical therapy for six months. I realized how lucky I was to be alive, and gained a new optimism. I wanted more than eighty percent function for the rest of my life. This inspired me to make a career and life change, and I studied and became a physical therapist.

Today I am a teacher for the interns in my center who are working towards their degrees as physical therapists. I encourage them to be the best they can be and to make a positive difference with their work attitude.

They watch me as I care for our patients, observing my satisfaction and gratitude. And now I inspire others as I was inspired years ago through my recovery and life-changing experience.

What a wake-up call that was! It changed me forever mentally, emotionally, and physically.

Each day I remember that all humans are basically good.

—Chris, making a difference as a kind therapist and inspiring teacher to his young protégés

DO WHAT YOU LOVE...
LOVE WHAT YOU DO

When I was in my thirties and living in San Francisco, I worked the graveyard shift at the post office. I was majoring in English and speech arts at San Francisco State University and working towards a degree in public administration.

One night I was having lunch with a coworker, who I knew worked two jobs. He asked if I would like a job as a teacher in the Adult Education program in San Carlos. He assured me that the twenty to thirty students all had ethnic backgrounds. I said sure, signed up, and accepted a class assignment.

As I was walking down the hall towards my assigned classroom, I began to wonder what in the world I was doing! I looked in the door's window at all the students waiting for me—the teacher—to arrive.

Well, I decided to go ahead. I walked into the classroom with no idea about what to do.

Somehow I connected with the students in special ways, and suddenly realized this was my career. I fell in love with teaching. It was 1970, and I was beginning my life-long career.

By 1975 I was teaching mid-level ESL to students from Vietnam. I was slowly gaining a reputation in Adult Education, and I became known to the local community colleges.

I believed it was about what you could do—not the authority of a piece of paper.

I began teaching communications, building reading skills, reading fundamentals at West Valley College, and then I transferred to Mission College.

I encouraged my students to remember that making a mistake is an opportunity to learn and can be fun.

Today, at age eighty-two, I am still teaching part-time at Mission College. My years of teaching and my love of words have helped me become a good writer. *I am a traffic director with ideas.*

And, I remember this wise saying: "Look for the light of humanity in everyone you meet."

I enjoy my retirement community and staying in touch with my daughters. It is good to remember that age is just a number.

—George, 82, an inspiring teacher, who has written and published his memoirs

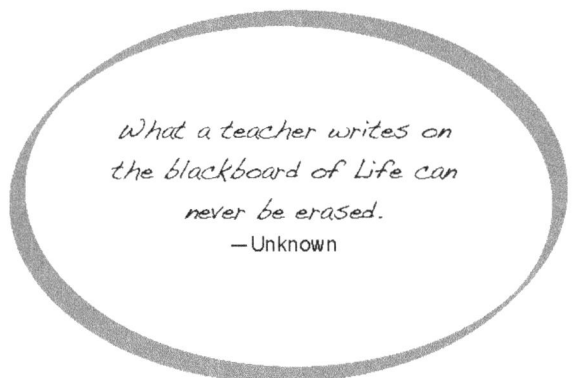

YOU CAN DO IT!

Forty-five years ago, Etta and I met. She was a Southern belle, and in her Southern drawl she invited me to go places with her. I rarely said no.

Etta was athletic, but she grew up with the idea that Southern ladies didn't sweat. She saw an article about a marathon race, thought it would be fun, signed up, and ran in it. At the finish line she gasped, "You are doing a marathon next year." I nodded, without much enthusiasm. I did, however, enter a 3.4-mile race, and there she was, cheering me on as I reached the finish line.

My mother lived in Hawaii, and there was to be marathon near her birthday. Of course, Etta gave me the usual, "You can do it, Louise!" And so that marathon became my goal, and I started running obsessively. One day I had to call home because my legs gave out. The chiropractor declared there would be no more marathons, and I couldn't stop sobbing.

Enter Etta. She took me and my X-rays to two doctors in the orthopedic department at the hospital. They prescribed rest and swimming, no running. So I swam, started to heal, and finally jogged. Could I do it? Etta was convinced that I could. My friend Jim gave me two small Menehune (Hawaiian mythological people) figurines to get me through the race. So off I went to Hawaii.

The local paper suggested wearing a fun sign on your back during the race. Mine read, "Louise says smile." As I raced by, people said, "Louise, I am smiling" or "Hi Louise."

Hawaiians at decorated booths every mile offered water and threw it on us to keep us cool. In the last six miles, I hurt everywhere but pretended I had a Menehune on each shoulder yelling, "You can do it!" like Etta.

And then the race was over, and I made it! Jim and friends cheered and threw leis around my neck. But I felt a bit of a let down. Was this it? I had been consumed by this goal for months. And my mother was unable to be at the finish because of the heat. The race took a lot out of me.

However, after the celebration and calls from home, I was jubilant. With such an accomplishment I decided I wanted "I did a marathon" etched on my tombstone. Many other races followed.

I owe a lot to Etta, who taught me I could do almost anything. Today her daughter cares for her. I discovered a way to be with her by reading children's books. She smiles, and in her Southern drawl says "Louise, thanks for coming." It is our ritual. I hug her, calling her "my Etta."

I will always hear her voice saying, "You can do it!" We all should have an Etta in our lives.

—*Louise, a happy writer, encouraging others in her memoirs class*

FOLLOW YOUR STAR!

All I ever wanted was to be a pilot!

I grew up in Chicago near Stagg Field where Enrico Ferme did his magic with the A-bomb development in the 1940s.

After high school I attended junior college for two years. The Korean War was on, and I was accepted into the Air Force Aviation Cadet Program. In 1951 I began pre-flight training, and we had our first flight in the AT-6 Texan, pre-jet training, flying the T-33 jet trainer, and the first jet fighter F-80.

In 1952 I received my commission and wings, and in 1953 we were fighter pilots off to Korea as replacement pilots in 67th FBS, flying the F-86 Saber. I flew ten missions before the truce was declared. My squadron went to France, and I completed my enlistment, flying the 86-H model Sabre until my release in 1955.

The job as squadron safety officer introduced me to accident investigation and confirmed my desire to become an engineer. With the GI bill I applied at the University of Illinois. Sadly, my two-year degree didn't apply, so I started over and got my degree in Aero Engineering in 1960. I accepted an offer with an aircraft company that turned out to be "make work," so I found another job as a sales person and field engineer at a high vacuum equipment company.

I went out west to California to a series of dead-end and high-pressure jobs that paid good money. I got back into aviation at Ames Research Center (NASA), working with cockpit instrumentation and human factors, and joined a USAF reserve unit flying C-119s and C-124s. I took a pay cut, but got back to flying. I needed to overcome the rejections that I was too old.

So, at thirty-six I finally got the greatest job in the world…flying! I retired at sixty but returned as a flight engineer for four years, with added income and perks. I was the oldest new hire ever—until the age restriction was removed.

I now encourage others to hang in there…no matter what! Follow your star, and do whatever it takes!

My sixth grade teacher said I wouldn't amount to much, since I just wanted to talk with others and look out the window. How well that turned into a career!

—*Bob, the busy and happily retired pilot*

UP, DOWN, AND BACK UP AGAIN

I was born—one of eight siblings–in a small town on the border of Mexico. My mother died when I was three; my father died when I was seven. At one point there were sixteen kids living with our grandparents. We lived on food stamps and Red Cross donations. Out of our eight siblings, two graduated from high school, and I was the only one to graduate from college.

During high school I worked selling newspapers and shining shoes, and I was salutatorian of my graduating class. A month after graduation I joined the Navy, served two years, and was honorably discharged. Then I got married and went to college under the GI Bill. I was accepted at Stanford University.

After graduating from Stanford and Stanford Medical School, I finished my residency in Ohio and accepted a vascular fellowship at the Veterans Hospital in Phoenix. I passed the American Board of Surgery exam, started a small practice, and four years later I became a Fellow of the American College of Surgeons. I was proud to be the first Latino general surgeon in Arizona.

I had a very successful general surgery practice for forty years, with patients from several states of Mexico. My patients included three Mexican governors and the nephew of the ruling President.

My children were born in different cities—wherever my training took me. I am very proud that they are well educated and professionally independent. They are judges, doctors, attorneys, and business professionals.

My wife became interested in medicine. She took pre-med courses and was accepted to the Indiana School of Medicine. Off we went to Indianapolis. There was a large Latino population and only one Hispanic doctor with a busy practice, so I opened a primary care practice. The goal was to work until my wife graduated, retire, and then hand over the practice to her.

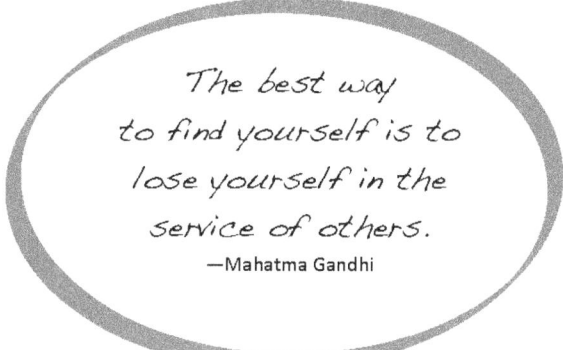

The best way to find yourself is to lose yourself in the service of others.
—Mahatma Gandhi

Then my personal life shattered. My wife divorced me, and I was confronted with heavy alimony and mounting debts. I thought I could manage with my retirement investments. Another blow came with the recession and a big loss of retirement money.

I felt I was reasonably healthy and couldn't retire, so I continued my practice from two to six each afternoon. I performed minor surgeries in the office. Ninety percent of my patients were Hispanics who appreciated that I spoke their language and understood their culture.

I accepted no insurance, took cash, and extended credit. I was aware of the poor economy and was happy to agree on fees. I was making a difference and enjoying my life as I worked my way back from losses and challenges.

—Humberto, a doctor devoted to his patients

HOW A FIRE STARTED MY CAREER

I grew up in Mountain View, California, across the street from the local fire station. As kids we were allowed to hang out there from time to time, and the firefighters were always friendly with us.

My first experience with a firefighter came when I was five years old. I had been playing with matches with the neighbor kids, and we'd set a part of the apple orchard on fire. When they arrived, a firefighter grabbed me by the scruff of my neck, read me the riot act, and threatened to send me to jail if I ever did something like that again.

Scared out of our wits, we were sent home awaiting punishment from our parents. But the firemen never told them, and I was forever grateful that my parents never found out we'd started the fire. Even at that young age, it was a life-changing experience; it led to my career as a firefighter.

Just out of high school, I worked in several areas of the automotive industry. I enjoyed the work, but I knew it was not meant to be my career. So I tested for a fire department position and joined in 1978.

In all these years there hasn't been a day when I didn't want to go to work. I can't say I have seen it all, but I have seen just about everything you might expect. And each day I never knew what might happen.

As time went on, I married and had a family, and the schedule allowed me to be home during some weekdays and have quality time with my wife and kids. I was always grateful to come home safely.

Today I work with a cross section of professionals from all walks of life. Nowadays, the fire department is more diverse with women firefighters, paramedics, and advanced care professionals.

Because we live and share forty-eight hours together each shift, coworkers become like our second families. As a crew, we depend upon each other and watch each other's back during an emergency. And we would trust each other with our lives if need be.

I believe that all the people at work, those I have met and cared for, and all the experiences I've had during my career have made me who I am today.

Pretty Lucky!

—Bruce, 50-something professional happily serving his community

TWO SOULS CROSSING PATHS

My story is one of recovery, connection, and community—with a heavy dose of serendipity in the mix.

In 1993 I hit bottom. I knew about AA, so I attended meetings, got a sponsor, worked the twelve steps, and got sober. I made the mistake of thinking I had arrived or graduated, so I left AA and relapsed. Getting and *staying* sober was more difficult.

I was approaching retirement from the fire department, and realized that my years as a firefighter/paramedic had been my refuge and that I needed a good recovery program. I returned to AA and my sponsor, and I attended meetings every day I wasn't working.

> *Important encounters are planned by the soul...long before the bodies see each other.*
> —Paul Coelho

One Friday we got a call from a local hotel regarding an unconscious young woman who had been binge drinking for a week. Almost unconscious, she had called friends who called 911. We arrived, took her vital signs and assisted her onto the gurney and into the ambulance.

That was it; it was an unremarkable 911 call I'd experienced many times—or so I thought. I felt deep empathy for her considering my four days of sobriety. On Monday when I was at a meeting, the same woman walked in and sat down in front of me.

I felt happy to see her, sad that she wasn't well, and I had a strong sense that something bigger than us was at play. I touched her shoulder, and said, "it is good to see you here." She turned with a look of mixed irritation and confusion, and I said, "I was one of the firefighters who helped you Friday."

Her expression turned to shock as she said, "Thank you, I guess."

"Thank you," I said. "I was four days sober that day, and helping you helped me."

That was six years ago, and we are friends today. As we got to know each other, I found out what that Monday had meant to her. She thought that God had sent me to her. I didn't know how big an impact I had made.

I can't really explain it, but in helping her that day we both experienced "a power greater than ourselves." It was just another 911 call, as well as a deeply spiritual and healing experience.

On our four-year sobriety anniversaries we met for breakfast, took pictures, and we both posted them on Facebook. Well, we found out her cousin is my sister's best friend, and her sister's children attend classes at my niece's gym. Strange small world connections!

What does all this mean? No idea. But we are two souls that crossed paths one day, and that connection was the beginning of a long and healing sobriety for both of us. What a blessing!

—Bill, retired firefighter, counting his blessings and sharing his stories

LET'S DANCE!

As a young woman in my early twenties in Hollywood, California, I was working at an insurance company and feeling very restless because I was not comfortable behind a desk in an office environment.

One day I met a young man who was a teacher at the Arthur Murray dance studio in Hollywood. He suggested that I become a dance instructor. He assured me the studio would train me in all the American and Latin dances, and it would be great fun. So, I went for an interview, became an instructor, and fell in love with the business.

The young man became my husband, and we opened a dance studio in Long Beach called "Miles of Dancing" because his first name was Miles. We had the studio for several years and then started a family, which, of course, changed our priorities. However, we continued to offer group and private lessons as a side business because we loved it so much.

Dancing has been such an important part of my life. It's allowed me to express myself through music and stay healthy through exercise. I have met so many wonderful people who have become my friends.

When the music starts... the feet will follow.
— Unknown

I am now eighty-two years old. I still teach ballroom dancing and feel blessed to be able to do it. I do have aches and pains sometimes, but as long as I can walk and talk, I will never give up. I will be dancing!

It is so important expressing ourselves in life doing something that we feel passionate about and keeping a positive attitude. *Stay healthy, have fun,* and *help others* are some of my mottos.

So whatever excites, intrigues, or brings you joy and fun—express yourself—it is never too late!

—*Marlene, a charming lady, still dancing and sharing stories*

GAGA, POPPOO...
AND MAE

I grew up in south central Los Angeles. I was an only child, and while my parents worked, I spent a lot of time with my grandparents, GaGa and Poppoo. I loved being with them, and in summer I would be at their house five days a week.

My grandparents lived in a single-family bungalow. Poppoo, who was a quiet man, built a garage, enclosed patio, work area, and a beautiful brick barbecue. Once, a kid down the block broke into his patio area and stole several radios and televisions. Fearlessly, he marched down the street, found the kid, and demanded, "Give back my stuff!" Everything was returned!

I was six when I came to know their next-door neighbor Mae. I got to play with her children, who were three and five. Mae dearly loved GaGa and enjoyed coming for coffee while GaGa regaled her with stories of Texas and how one must be a refined and genteel woman—like GaGa. Mae was a very vibrant lady, with such a love of life. She was always smiling. I would see her through my grandparents' kitchen window coming out her back door. I would run out, giggle, and say, "Hi Mae."

I never thought of her as a mom—just a very special friend.

Well, as the neighborhood changed, Mae and her husband decided to move to southwest Los Angeles. Sadly, what had been a close-knit family community changed to a drug- and gang-infested neighborhood. But Mae never left us behind. She would come and visit GaGa and invite me over to sleep in the bunk beds with her girls. I always felt loved and included.

I was thirteen when she started teaching me life lessons with such sayings as "Never take advice from someone whose life you do not admire."

I am now fifty-six and remain in contact with Mae, who is seventy-seven. She often reminds me about how I would giggle and say "hi Mae" with my big grin.

For fifty years Mae has been a source of inspiration, wisdom, love, and kindness. She has been a great mentor, and I feel blessed by the role she has played in my life.

How wonderful when we have wise people to guide us through our lives. And, they are all around us if we just take the time to look, listen, and giggle!

—Lori, a gracious spiritual being passing on what she has learned

THE MANY TWISTS AND TURNS ON THE WAY TO BECOMING A TEACHER

I was born in a little town in Michigan to two kind parents. At birth, my neck and back were damaged, and as a child I felt left out of playing, so I entertained myself by drawing.

My parents found a great osteopathic doctor. I had a surgery, and my back was healed.

This gave me a whole new lease on life.

I was an average student until high school, and I began to realize that I was gay. There was no "coming out." However, I did well in high school, and I was offered a Congressional Scholarship to the American University in Washington, D.C.

It was 1941, and we were involved in the war. So I went to Wayne University, Michigan, and in my senior year I worked part time in insurance while I studied Special Education. Unfortunately, I broke my elbow, and I was not allowed in the classroom with my arm in a sling.

So I went back to the insurance company and worked full time while I finished my degree in evening classes. Then I experienced another turn on the road…a program with the insurance company moved me to San Francisco.

Another twist: after the war—in 1948 I was drafted into the Army. In 1949 I came back home, and six months later was in the reserves. The Korean War began, and I was processing the paperwork for servicemen at Letterman Hospital.

Then back to work in insurance. I began to ask myself, "Do I want to do this for the rest of my life?" When I was going to be relocated to Portland, I quit.

It was the early 1950s. I met my first partner, got my credentials, and began teaching handicapped children how to live independently. Finally I was teaching!

Another life surprise…I met Ginny (another teacher), we became friends, and during Christmas vacation we married. We shared twenty-five years of friendship and happiness until her passing. I was happy teaching for thirty-plus years, and now I enjoy retirement.

There were many twists and turns on the way to my happiness as a teacher. And I shared my life with partners who were first and foremost my friends.

Today, at ninety-one…I am beginning a new life in a new place with a new partner…a vineyard!!

The moral of the story…accept setbacks, keep your eye on your dream, appreciate friendship where you find it, and keep your heart open to contentment and peace.

—*Dean, a charming 91-year-young adventurer*

LOOKING BACK AT 105

I grew up in Calabria, a small village in southern Italy. Each year Papa went to work on the railroad in Canada and in the northern United States. And every year he came home, and Mama got pregnant. One day Mama laid down the law. "That's it," she said. "No more going to America without us."

So arrangements were made, we were sad to say goodbye to our grandparents, whom we might never see again. My little brother Peter cried, "I will die if I go to America," and he died after we arrived. Somehow he knew.

It was a long, rough boat ride with the men above and the women and children below. We met every day. The thrill of coming into the New York harbor and seeing the Statue of Liberty made up for it.

We stayed on Ellis Island in a big room as they checked our health, and we got cleaned up. Then they called our names, and we were welcomed to America!

We took a train to California, and since there were few seats, we took turns sitting and standing. We arrived in Hollister with $5, and moved in with relatives in a very crowded house.

The local cannery burned down. That created lots of work, so my parents and sister Virginia got jobs. Mr. Felice fixed up part of a barn for us. Later when things were better, we got two railroad cars to live in. We were comfortable and clean. I took care of the young ones.

I tried to go to school, but I was twelve and didn't know English. Aunt Isabel taught me how to read and write, and I learned English, Spanish, and some Portuguese. We didn't have toys, so we made our own dolls. Mama and Virginia made our dresses, and once in a while we got shoes.

On Saturday nights there was a party with music and food. Mama and Papa sang, and everyone danced. It was wonderful. During the week we baked bread in a backyard oven, grew vegetables, and raised chickens for eggs and meat.

The boys picked grapes, tomatoes, and prunes, and sold lettuce or swept out stores. Everyone worked.

There were seven of us: Virginia, John, Irene, Peter II, Joey, Carla, and me. Irene and Carla went to beauty college, became hairdressers, and fixed hair; they duplicated the styles of the movie stars!

I met and married Joe at age twenty. Mama and Virginia made the dress; Irene made the headpiece. We had three sons—Philip, Eugene, and Donald—all born at home. Joe was always at my side, doing the chores and letting me rest. I ended up helping to raise Virginia's children, as well.

Joe had a job at the high school for more than twenty years. He retired with a nice pension. I worked at the cannery until retirement age. We did well and bought our first house in 1962, where I still live.

In the 1950s several moved away, and only Virginia and I remained in Hollister. We missed the rest so much. It was never the same after that.

It is amazing what families can accomplish and endure when they stick together. My life has been full of adventure, hard work, and lots of laughter and love.

And it would make me so happy having my family all together at least one more time.

—Angelina, 105, an amazing lady with a story of the American dream

HOW A VISIT TURNED A LIFE AROUND

I was just a young police officer when I received a call from a distraught father asking for ideas and guidance for his young son, then about age twelve. He said his son was getting into trouble and was having challenges with school and other kids.

Clearly, the father loved and cared for the safety of this young man. I suggested that he and his son come down for a tour of the police department and meet and talk with some of the officers, and so they did. Well, you never know how your concern and your words are heeded or ignored by young people.

Three years ago the same father called and proudly told us that his son had become a police officer. He was a small town police chief in Texas. I immediately looked him up on the internet and sent him a "way to go" message.

—*Anonymous career police officer*

LET ME ENTERTAIN YOU

My parents were both in the Army, stationed in California when they were expecting their first child. My mom went to visit family in Tennessee, and while she was there, I was born. They called me her "vacation baby."

When I was in the sixth grade, my dad became a pastor in a church in a small town nearby, and I attended school in portable classrooms. I was the only black child in this town of Spanish-speaking families. They had no track team, so I started running, entered the finals in a regional meet, and took third place for my school.

I was popular and always chose talking over fighting when it came to solving problems. I was offered several scholarships to private schools, but chose to stay in my own school district. In high school I did well. I was very athletic, and became the director of the talent show in my junior and senior years. I loved it! I wanted to be a performer.

Where words fail, music speaks.
—Hans Christian Andersen

During high school I had a son, and I married his mother when I was eighteen. I had to shift my priorities from basketball to work, and I took a job as a driver and sales rep for Pepsi-Cola. I continued working, we had two more sons, and I enjoyed singing in the church choir and performing at events. We were then living in San Jose.

My dad passed away in 1992, and I was going through a divorce, so I went back to stay with my mom over the holidays. By then I owned a distributorship with a snack company, and in 1996 the company was closed. With my severance I began computer training, but my love was music.

So, my sons and I moved back to Watsonville to live with Mom and find ways to give my music a chance. I began singing and performing in parades and at events and was invited to the Blues Festival, where I did the vocals for a blues band that opened for James Brown.

I was performing, running my own limousine service, and sleeping only three or four hours a night.

And then one day I went to get up and knew something was wrong. I needed help. I called 911, and the ambulance took me to Valley Medical Hospital, where I passed out and went into a coma in the emergency room. I had a sense of hearing the following phrase:

We are sparing your life, so go and share the miracle through your performing.

I was in the hospital for two months, and since I had a bubble in my heart, I needed to reduce all stress. Then a surgery at that hospital saved my life.

Today I am partnered with that same hospital, organizing and performing at fundraisers to increase awareness to prevent diabetes in children.

I am a Barry White impersonator performing around the world.

—Kenny, living in gratitude for his miracle

YOU STEP INTO YOUR POWER WHEN YOU HIT THE DRUM

My life began in 1950 in Marin County. I was a Japanese-American child, born with a free spirit and great confidence. There were few Asians at that time in my hometown, and in kindergarten I met with prejudice for the first time.

My self-esteem was dashed, and feelings of rejection caused me to become withdrawn. My schoolmates made me feel that I represented the Japanese race, and I was the enemy. I didn't understand my Japanese-American identity, and I felt a sense of self-hatred. I didn't even want to be seen with my own relatives. All I wanted was to be accepted.

In my high school senior year I started getting some social consciousness. It was the time of the Vietnam War, which I felt was wrong.

I enrolled at Cal State Hayward and asked myself, "What should I become? Should I major in math? Computer science?" I was introduced to Asian-American Studies, and it was my first opportunity to address my Asian-American identity.

So, at nineteen I took the class and did a paper on the internment camps in the United States during WWII. I interviewed my parents, and learned about their experiences. I came to understand their reserve and desire to protect me. They would say, "Don't stand out; be quiet." I was still seeking my identity. *Who am I?*

I transferred to Berkeley, and in 1972 I graduated with a degree in Social Sciences. Off I went to Japan. I wanted to find my Japanese roots, but I found I wasn't accepted there, either. They didn't understand seeing an American in a Japanese body.

When I returned to the U.S., I heard about a Taiko group that formed at the Buddhist church to attract young people back to the church. As soon as I heard Taiko being played I said, "Oh wow! I want to do that! I want to be loud and unabashed!"

I realized that women could be as powerful as men on stage, and once I played, I became infused with the rapture of vibration. Taiko is a sport, martial art, dance, and music ensemble, with amazing camaraderie. It is a transforming activity where I can be bombastic in body, mind, and spirit.

I had felt displaced and lost, and was looking to connect and have a sense of purpose. Now I make a difference through training, performing…while maintaining and preserving this culture. You step into your power when you hit the drum!

There is such joy in supporting others to step into their potential, to share, and find their joy.

At age twenty-three with Taiko I found my voice!

—*PJ, a caring woman, hitting the Taiko drum with great power and joy*

IF YOU WANT IT...FIND THE WAY!

My husband worked, and I was home caring for our three children. My dream was to take our family to see Europe. When my husband said it was not possible with his income, I replied "What if I get a job and save for our trip?"

Good man. He agreed.

So when our children were in school all day, I attended university for a teaching credential. I learned that teachers were paid by their degrees. I got my masters, and I taught elementary school while saving my salary.

First, our daughter wanted to go to France with her French teacher. Then, finally, in 1970 my two sons, then thirteen and seventeen, and I took an eight-week trip using Eurail passes.

We visited France, Switzerland, Austria, Italy, Germany, Denmark, Netherlands, and Belgium. We bicycled on dikes in Holland, skied the Matterhorn in Switzerland, and toured the Rhine River.

Then we met my husband in London and spent three weeks touring England, Scotland, Wales, and Ireland. Our oldest son took pictures, and our youngest made a scrapbook along the way.

We all love traveling and have enjoyed many trips through the years. And this gave our sons a great interest in photography and history.

I had a dream, and I went out and found the way!

—Margaret, 90, wrote two books about her mom and dad

I ALWAYS WANTED TO BE A DOCTOR

Growing up in India, I knew I wanted to be a doctor at an early age. So I finished college in Bombay, however, I had my heart set on coming to America. My mother and the family agreed, and she provided the money for me.

In those days young women from India did not travel alone, and certainly not halfway around the world without family or introductions. I had written to the Church Home and Hospital in Baltimore, Maryland, and received a fellowship to John Hopkin's Hospital. I studied pathology with Dr. Woodruff and Dr. Novak, and endocrinology at the University of Maryland.

I was on my way to becoming a doctor!

I remained in America, finished my medical training, and was introduced to a young man whose family my sister knew in India. He was living and working in New Jersey, so I flew there to meet him. I decided that he was okay! So we fell in love, got married, and I worked at the Robert Wood Johnson Hospital in Hamilton, New Jersey.

Well, I decided I wanted to practice as an OBGYN doctor. During that time I had a son and brought many other babies into the world in New Jersey. I was a doctor there until I retired at age sixty-five. Then I moved to California when I was seventy-five.

I was quite an adventurer for my time, going to another country at such a young age.

I had my heart set on medical school in America, and becoming a doctor, and so I followed my dream. We all have dreams throughout our lives, and it is so wonderful to make them come true!

—*Vasant, 75, happily retired in Priya Living Community*

TRINIDAD MAMA

I was born and raised on the island of Trinidad. We were poor, but we took care of each other. My dad spent time away at clubs, and my mom worked. I attended only elementary school, and I grew up, as my brother and I took care of the young kids.

Later on I met a man. We had a baby boy, and lived together for seven years, both working in merchandising. He began working on cruise ships when our son was three, which provided a better income. Then one day I overheard him telling a friend that he met a woman he was going to marry. Sadly he left with all our money, so I returned to work, and with the help of my family we took good care of my son. He had lots of people looking out for him.

My brother got hired on a cruise ship, and things got better. Now my son was five and going to school. And I began to pray to God to send me a nice man. Well, as it turned out, I met my husband in a band at Carnival. We fell in love, got married, and two years later had our daughter.

This year we have been married eighteen years, and I so appreciate this good man.

Now my son was fifteen and wanted to come to his dad and family in the U.S. So my baby boy left and made a new life, and I am so proud of him. He continued his education, and graduated from university with a degree in marketing. And he went on to build a successful business as a social media and marketing consultant.

So I, Trinidad Mama, got my green card so I could visit my son and family in the U.S. One by one and two by two our whole family will be coming back together in the new homeland.

> Di Olda Di Moon
> Di Brighta It shine.
> (Age brings wisdom.)
> —Unknown

What did I learn from all of this? To take care of those you love, and let go of regrets and disappointments. No matter how rich or poor, family is precious, and it does take a village to raise all our children.

—Joan, a true island mama with a big laugh and bigger hugs

PRECIOUS MOMENTS

I have been thinking about so many precious moments and memories from my family.

MOM:
When I was a very little girl, I was allowed to walk the two blocks from our apartment to the corner to meet my mom as she was getting off the streetcar coming home from work. Each day I cherished that time we had together walking back home hand in hand, me sharing my day with her.

DAD:
Each week there was a precious moment on Friday. My dad traveled for work from Monday to Friday, and I would wait by the front door of our apartment, on the third floor, to hear him coming up the stairs. I would race down to meet him, and as tired as he might be, he would reach in his pocket and find some money so we could have an ice cream cone together.

While we celebrate the big events, it is so important to treasure those little moments with others, so we have a wonderful and full memory box after they are gone.

Don't email, phone, or text. Go visit. We have to be present to get the great stuff like hugs, kisses, and smiles.

—*Danni, the vintage woman*

ACKNOWLEDGEMENTS

ANGEL SPONSORS:

The Mlnarik Law Group Inc.
www.mlnariklaw.com

Kathy and Karl Winkelman
Senior Care Authority

Vicky Tsai, Owner
Dry Clean Pro, Santa Clara

Campbell Physical Therapy
Campbell, CA

ANGEL SUPPORTERS:

LocalBizNet
Help and Care LLC

Nora Monette, George Myers, Ubaldo and Helen Baldovinos, Mark and Dahlia Sheperd, Lilly Yen, Jim Oggerino, Chuck Chaffin, Louise Webb, Mel Irvin, Quacy Superville, Dean Gross, Lori Gibson Washington

David, Clyde, Jean, several residents at Priya Living, and all those who supported us anonymously.

Thank you for listening, cheering, contributing, and believing in me and the value of this book.

ABOUT THE AUTHOR

Danni grew up in a Scottish Canadian family of storytellers, and was intrigued by history and stories from around the world. So, after college she began an adventure living in five countries, visiting many others, and gaining knowledge, skills, and a deep respect for different cultures.

She returned to California, worked for fifteen years in HR, as a recruiter, trainer, and manager. She became a certified graphologist, which enhanced her understanding of the uniqueness and diversity of people.

And, then it was time to begin her own consulting business as a speaker, trainer, and mentor.

She had a foot in two worlds: business and education. She was a visiting professor in colleges and universities, and she enjoyed working with businesses. Her seminars have been presented to hundreds of multi-generational and multi-cultural audiences in corporate meeting rooms, college classrooms, and large auditoriums.

During these thirty years she achieved certifications in International Career Coaching, NLP Master Training and Master in Advanced Language Skills.

Today Danni's work is Business Theatre, the art of educating, inspiring, and entertaining.

Through her Speak Easy Events her clients enhance their skills with stories, humor, metaphors and improv.

And, yes, she is the vintage Scottish storyteller!

www.ingramcontent.com/pod-product-compliance
Lightning Source LLC
Chambersburg PA
CBHW070936160426
43193CB00011B/1697